Should KARGIL be an Election Issue?

Dr. Janak Raj Jai
Advocate
Supreme Court of India

RP
Regency Publications
New Delhi

The comments and information published in this book are solely of the Author, and the Publisher may or may not agree with them.

ISBN 81-87498-05-6

Published by Regency Publications, 20/36-G, Old Market, West Patel Nagar, New Delhi 110 008 and printed at Radiant Printers, New Delhi 110 008, Phones: 574 0038, 571 2539 • Telefax: 578 3571.

www.regencypublications.com
Email: *regency@satyam.net.in* and *info@regencypublications.com*

CONTENTS

INTRODUCTION

The battle of bullet at Kargil is over with the pronouncement of elections to the Lok Sabha and the Legislative Assemblies in the country; the battle of ballot has started in a big way. The model code of conduct has come into force, the day the elections were declared by the Election Commission of India. But who cares for the Code of Conduct.

The main Poll issue before all the political parties seems to be "Kargil" and the intelligence failure of the government. Political parties have started sharpening their knives against each other, and are bent upon fighting the ballot war bringing Kargil, intelligence failure, the blood of Jawans, and the agonies of their families on the streets. The care-taker government on whom the war of Kargil was thrust unexpectedly, successfully handled the situation and had been able to throw out the Pakistani Army Soldiers and the mercenaries from the Indian Soil. Not only this, the care-taker government earned worldwide appreciation for their measured restraint and patience. The United States of America, Britain, China, Russia, France, Germany and many more countries praised the Indian Government's wisdom and statesmanship in tackling the Kargil intrusion. In a letter addressed to our Prime Minister, the British Premier Mr. Tony Blair commended India's restraint in Kargil. The American President, Mr. Bill Clinton played a significant role to persuade Nawaz Sharif to withdraw their forces from Kargil and respect Line of Control. At the G-8 Meet, the French Ambassador is on record to say that "the Indian Prime Minister has been very wise in taking the position he has. The Indian Armed forces are doing very well in clearing the Indian side of the LOC.

Therefore, every Indian should be proud of this caretaker government, which has handled the Kargil crisis so wisely and has won worldwide appreciation. But the moot question before all of us today is whether Kargil should be an Election issue in the ensuing elections? Should the ruling party be allowed to take advantage of the victory in the Kargil crisis, and should we allow the opponent political parties to politicise the sacrifices of the Jawans and their families, on account of the alleged intelligence failure of the government. The answer lies with the people and the Indian voter. It may be in fitness of things to mention here that the Prime Minister of India, might in his speech at the Red Fort on 15th August, warn his partymen not to politicise the Kargil victory to cash votes, and at the same time appeal to all other political parties not to belittle the sacrifices of the Jawans by making Kargil an Election issue.

It will be quite relevant here to mention that the intelligence failure is not a new phenomena. There are many occasions when there had been an utter intelligence failure. Chinese aggression of 1962, was the biggest intelligence failure, operation blue star had to be conducted with the help of the Army on account of intelligence failure, and many more similar occasions arose when there was an intelligence failure on the part of earlier governments. But there is no use opening a pandora's box. This will not be good for the health of our country. It would be quite useful and informative for all those who wish to make Kargil an election issue, to read the following paragraphs on 1962 debacle taken out of the book "My Life and All That" written by Shri M.C. Setalvad, the then Attorney General of India.

"In the months of October and November 1962, India suffered a grave military disaster, which shook the complacent Stewardship of the Country by Nehru to its very foundations. The swift and sharp aggression by China on our north-eastern frontier which drove her armies 160 miles deep into Indian Territory almost without opposition nearly destroyed the supreme confidence which the Indian people had so far reposed in Nehru. The errors and omissions of his China Policy **were unforgivable blunders**. The then President of India was constrained to observe that "**we have been negligent and credulous**."

But nobody can doubt the integrity of Jawaharlal Nehru. He had been the darling of the Indian people and made unmatched sacrifices in the freedom struggle of the country. The Chinese aggression virtually broke him down, and he died as a sad man within less than two years of the Chinese aggression.

Taking into consideration all these events that took place within a span of fifty years, we have to calmly and dispassionately think and ponder whether such type of sensitive national security and intelligence failure matters should be discussed and debated on the streets during the elections. Some over-enthusiastic and unscrupulous people for their vested interests are bound to take advantage of this situation, the consequences of which will be disastrous for the country.

A major political party has come out with their political agenda saying that Kargil will be made a Poll issue in the ensuing elections. According to them the crown of glory for the Kargil victory belongs only to the forces, and not the caretaker Prime Minister. According to them the main thrust of their party will be on the intelligence failure of the government. A special Kargil cell has been opened. I quote from India today (August 9, 1999).

"The special Kargil cell of the Congress—headed by CWC member Pranab Mukherji and comprising K. Natwar Singh, Sibal and Mani Shankar Iyer—has been meeting daily, sometimes even twice a day to calibrate the party's response, "We have accepted the BJP's challenge and will take the issue from village to village", says CWC Member Rajesh Pilot.

Similarly BJP might also have opened some cell to cash the votes, on their victory in Kargil war. Some other parties must have opened Kargil cells for vested interests. The ill-informed and illiterate voter is certainly going to be utterly confused by such type of political acrobats. Their main problem is food, shelter and employment. But who bothers for the real problems faced by the general public. The main aim of the political parties is to win the election, even at the cost of the blood of the Jawans.

Taking clue from their masters that Kargil is going to be the main poll issue; some over-enthusiastic workers have started working on these lines, even if it means belittling the

Jawans and their families. I came across an article in Hindustan Times of 27th June 1999, under the caption "Who is belitting the troops?". The following paragraph will show that for BJP and Congress our soldiers' blood is merely a political tool.

"The Sheer Brazenness took one's breath away. There, in the icy heights of Kargil, our soldiers are dying in numbers that should shame us, playing with their lives for intelligence failures, administrative incompetence and complacent policy-making. Here, in the comfortable plains, we are being told not to cross-examine the government, the minister, the past, the future, because we must all stand together lest we demoralise the troops. Don't politicise the conflict, post mortems must wait. Being good citizens, we agree.

But when we opened our newspapers on Wednesday, what did we see?

We saw an advertisement which said, "More than a hundred of our soldiers have laid down their lives in the battle for Kargil." The names of some of them were printed and, below, was the BJP lotus. In a corner, in the humblest print possible, was the apologetic line, "Issued by Bharatiya Janata Party." How wonderful, we thought, the ruling party paying such touching homage to the martyrs.

Why haven't the BJP's opponents reacted to this audacious attempt to gain electoral mileage out of a national crisis and, in hundreds of homes, a personal tragedy? The Congress spokesman did make a mute protest, but he lacked conviction, didn't he?

For, the previous day, one of his own partymen had placed an advertisement. This worthy, going by the name of Ramesh Handa, used a stirring graphic of three silhouetted soldiers atop a hill unfurling the Tricolour, with a poem in Hindi alongside extolling the sacrifices of the Mother's brave sons. No prizes for guessing who the "Mother" is: Sonia Gandhi, of course, smiling with folded hands from one corner of the ad.

The Congress' only defence can be that, unlike the BJP, the party has not officially issued that ad. It is clearly the work of an over-enthusiastic sycophant, and nowhere does the name of the party of its electoral symbol figure. But that is just a quibble, for the association is unmistakable. If the Congress' motives were pure, it should have immediately disowned this ad and even threatened Handa with disciplinary action. Indeed, the reprimand should have come from Sonia Gandhi herself, for the ad clearly attempts to identify her with the upsurge in patriotic sentiment.

The Election Commission of India should take serious note of such things, and see that no one, howsoever high or low he/she may be, dares to play with the sacrifices of the Jawans, and their families, for seeking advantage in his favour in the elections. Such type of cheap tactics are indeed grave violations of the Model Code of Conduct. It is high time the Chief Election Commissioner acted and showed his mettle in order to conduct free and fair elections.

It is with this background that I thought of immediately bringing out a small book posing a serious question before all the peace loving citizens, whether Kargil should be made an election issue which almost all the political parties are inclined to do, for their vested interests. The book contains the handling of the Kargil situation by the care-taker government, the worldwide support to Indian strategy and diplomacy, political mudslinging against each other by the parties, earlier intelligence failures, author's letter to the Chief Election Commissioner, expert opinions on whether Kargil should be made an election issue, some editorials and letters to the editor.

I show my gratitude to all those whose material I have used for the larger benefit of the people. I also show my gratitude to Shri Y.P. Singh, Brigadier Mahindra Singh, Kewal Krishan Sharma and Shri Avtar Singh Sohal, my colleagues at the Bar, who have contributed articles for the book. The real credit of this book goes to my publisher, Shri Arun Kumar Verma, who showed more interest than the author, in bringing out this book in a week's time. His valuable advice and suggestions came very handy.

August 9, 1999
C-50, Rajpur Khurd Colony
Sewa Sadan
New Delhi 110068
Ph. 693 2057, 680 3447

Dr. Janak Raj Jai
Advocate, Supreme Court of India
L-II/68, Lajpat Nagar
New Delhi 110 024

AUTHOR'S LETTER

Letter dated 21-7-1999 addressed to The Chief Election Commissioner of India

Nirvachan Sadan
Parliament Street
New Delhi

Sir,

The applicant is an enlightened person, social activist, senior citizen, and humble son of the soil.

The Election Commission of India has declared elections for the Parliament and the Legislative Assemblies throughout the country. The code of conduct, therefore, comes into force from the date of announcement of the election. It is a coincidence that the country had to fight a battle at Kargil to flush out the intruders from the Indian soil. The whole country was united in this sacred duty to defend the motherland from the bad design of the enemy.

Now that the election process has started the political parties have brought the Kargil issue on the stress, visibly for their vested interests. One party wishes to take advantage of the victory at the Kargil whereas the other political parties are bent upon bringing disaffection among the people of the country by maligning the ruling party for the intelligence failure thereby demoralising the armed forces.

Washing dirty linen on the streets by making a poll issue on Kargil will not do any good to the health of democracy and the morale of the jawans, who are the real saviours of the borders of the country. If we keep on discussing Kargil on political platforms, we shall be opening a pandora's box. This mean and cheap type of mudslinging on political platforms is certainly in gross violation of the code of conduct issued by the Election Commission of India. Has the political leadership become so bankrupt that they have nothing to offer to the people except creating disaffection among them by making Kargil a major poll issue?

I therefore, on behalf of the citizens of the country, particularly the jawans and their families, most humbly make a fervent appeal to you Sir, to immediately issue strict and specific directions for all the political parties to keep Kargil out of their political agenda. Any delay in the matter will do an irreparable damage to the basic democratic structure of the country which is bound to jeopardise the very independence of the country earned with the blood of thousands of martyrs.

Yours faithfully

Dr. Janak Raj Jai

Note: The Election Commission of India, have not so far even acknowledged this letter addressed to the Commission.

Author

DEBACLE OF 1962

Those who are crying from the top hill that there has been an utter intelligence failure to protect Kargil from enemy's intrusion are doing no good either to themselves, or to the country as also to the Army personnel who are the saviours of our borders. They keep awake twenty-four hours, while the whole country sleeps in peace on their account.

Unfortunately the political parties are bent upon gaining mileage by projecting that the government failed to protect the Kargil from the enemy because of intelligence failure. The Congress Party demanded that the government should come clean on the circumstances leading to the armed intrusion in Kargil and claiming that lives of several hundreds of Jawans could have been saved if vigil on the Indo-Pak Border was not overlooked after the Lahore Declaration. To grill the government, the Congress Party went to the President to ask the Prime Minister, to convene a Rajya Sabha Session. Their sole object was to embarrass the government to the maximum, and humiliate them publicly, so that the Indian voter throws them out of power in the coming elections.

Even the West-Bengal Chief Minister, Jyoti Basu, who endorsed the demand for the Rajya Sabha Session had suggested that the Rajya Sabha Session should be convened after the intruders have been pushed out beyond the Line of Control.

The Five Member Delegation, which met the President included former Union Minister, Balram Jhakhar, Ahmad Patel, former Chief Justice of India Ranganath Mishra, Vayalar Ravi and Urmilabhen Patel. It is unfortunate that a retired Chief Justice of India should have taken keen interest in active politics and sided a particular political party. This type of step or activity by a retired Chief Justice of India, shall certainly weaken the faith of the people in the independence and impartiality of the Indian Judicial System. Nowhere the Congress Party has denounced Pakistna's bad designs for their intrusions, but they have all along been harping on one point—intelligence failure of the Government. This is a very shameful act on the part of the major opposition political party.

The Government did call an All Party Meet, as also the Chief Ministers Conference to apprise all the political parties, as to what steps are being taken to tackle the Kargil instrusion. Sonia Gandhi, was conspicuously absent in the All Party Meet. And the Congress party, particularly was not happy and satisfied with the Chief Ministers Conference. The Statesman of 6th July, 1999, carries a story on the anguish of Congress and other parties who were not satisfied with the Chief Ministers Conference and were adamant on their stand for a Rajya Sabha Session. I quote:

"The Congress and CPI-M demanded a Rajya Sabha Session on Kargil—the latter threatening "other measures", if the Government did not accede soon and the former marching to the President seeking a directive for the government to convene the Upper House.

A meeting of Chief Ministers (scheduled for 7th July) for briefings to parties by Prime Minister cannot substitute for a discussion in Parliament, said the Congress.

The Congress was particularly outraged that a "caretaker" regime should unilaterally take crucial wartime decisions. "The Rajya Sabha is the only elected body at a time when there is a caretaker government which has lost a confidence vote on the floor of the House, and is not answerable to any political party, or people's representatives", Dr. Jogi said.

In Chennai, the CPI-M Politburo Member, Mr. Prakash Karat gave Mr. Atal Bihari Vajpayee time till 7th July to convene a special session of the House of Elders, failing which the opposition would "get it convened through other measures". "A battle with high casualties could not be left to a defeated caretaker government", Mr. Karat said.

The CPI-M leader hit out at the government's "flawed" nuclear and Strategic policies—the seeds of Kargil lay in the Pokhran blasts of last year, he said, and declared that nuclearisation had led India "to play into the hands of Pakistan".

In Bagalk at Bijapur, the Congressman Mr. Ghulam Nabi Azad announced India had lost its image in the international Community because the government had "failed to stop" the intrusions.

1962 Debacle: All those who had been and have been criticising the Vajpayee government for their failure to protect the Kargil from the enemy intrusion must read M.C. Sitalvad's book "My life and all that". They will get complete answer to their shallow criticism on the handling of the Kargil problem by the Government. I quote from Sitalvad's book one or two paragraphs (pp 483-484):

"In the months of October and November 1962, India suffered a grave military disaster, which shook the complacent stewardship of the country by Nehru to its very foundations. The swift and sharp aggression by China on our north-eastern frontier which drove her armies 160 miles deep into Indian territory almost without opposition very nearly destroyed the Supreme Confidence which the Indian People had so far reposed in Nehru. The errors and omissions of his China Policy **were unforgivable blunders**. The then President of India was constrained to observe that **"We have been Negligent and Credulous."**

On the 7th October, 1950, the Chinese Liberation Army had marched into Tibet. Far-seeing men in Indian Political life had then realised the great danger which India would have to face by the march of China into Tibet. We would have a powerful neighbour on our northern Himalayan Boundary. Nehru, trusting the glib protestations of friendship and peaceful action by the Chinese, failed to perceive this danger in spite of a weighty warning from his colleagues in the government. On 7th November 1950, Sardar Patel had written to him a detailed letter, pointing out with powerful reasons what it would mean to India to have China as her northern neighbour. Among the many other problems which he thought had arisen by reason of Chinese' action in Tibet, one may be quoted:

"My own feeling is that unless we are sure of our supply of arms, ammunition and armour, we would be making our defence position perpetually weak, and we would not be able to stand up to the double threat of difficulties both from the west and north-west.

Sardar Patel died soon after his admonition, and warning which, along with others, remained unweded. Blindly wedded to his own theory, that China was a friend and misled by our first Ambassador at Peking, Panikkar and other advisors, Nehru ignored the warning which was written large on the wall and was obvious to many military men. China followed up its action in Tibet by patrolling in the Ladakh area in 1951. Even this action did not wean away Nehru from his settled policy.

To quote his own words uttered later in Parliament, "I saw no reason to discuss the frontiers with the Chinese government because foolishly, if you like, I thought there was nothing to discuss". Choosing men who would fall with his views he had installed as the Defence Minister Krishna Menon who held that port-folio from 1957 to 1962. The Minister remained completely oblivious to the growing danger and India was completely unprepared to meet what many had considered a distinct probability.

Intelligence Failure: It was not surprising, therefore, that when China attacked us on 20th October, 1962, not only were we completely unprepared, but our intelligence had failed to inform us of the vast infantry and artillery forces which had been massed by the Chinese against our north-eastern border. The plains of Assam lay at the mercy of the invading Chinese forces, and, but for the sudden and unilateral decision of the Chinese to withdraw on 20th November, 1962, Assam would have been overrun.

Most naturally, the people rose unitedly in revolt against the Defence Minister who had landed the Country into this disaster. They were in no mood to listen Nehru when he tried to save him. Squarely Nehru's party gave him the bitter choice of discarding Menon or relinquishing Premiership. Forced thus by irresistible public opinion to give up his favourite, Nehru once the hero of Indian people, lost his prestige and was himself a disillusioned man. Indeed it is sad that the Chinese aggression was the real cause of his physical breakdown, which resulted in his death less than two years later. (Sitalvad was the Attorney General of India, and had also been the Chairman, Law Commission of India).

Note: This writer had the good fortune of having worked closely with Prime Minister Jawaharlal Nehru, being a member of his personal staff. After the Chinese aggression in 1962, Jawaharlal virtually broke down. I saw him often sitting underneath his favourite tree at the Prime Minister's House for hours in a melancholy mood. This aggression was perhaps the biggest blow to his life, in his political career.

It is distressing that no lessons were learnt from the Chinese aggression of 1962. In fact all the governments after Jawaharlal Nehru failed to strengthen the country militarily. Amazingly, all the opponent political parties particularly the Congress Party, have now the cheeks to criticise the present caretaker government, and are bent upon pinning down the government on Kargil crisis, by making it a Poll issue in the ensuing elections.

Worldwide Support to India on Kargil Handling

It is a matter of great comfort and relief that the way the Kargil crisis has been handled by the government, it has earned worldwide appreciation. Diplomatically and strategically, India has gained considerably internationally.

Even China drew itself closer to the views of the International community on Kargil. The diplomatic isolation of Pakistan is likely to deepen. To a specific question on the current Indo-pak tensions, in Kargil, a spokesman of the Chinese Ministry of Foreign Affairs said in Beijing, "We sincerely hope that both India and Pakistan earnestly respect the line of Control in Kashmir." This is the first time since the unfolding of the Kargil confrontation that China has made a specific reference to respecting the LOC which has been violated by Pakistan. Coming barely a day after Prime Minister, Nawaz Sharif concluded his talks with the Chinese leaders, Beijing's new affirmation on the LOC might cause deep disappointment in Islamabad. It has been observed that the new Chinese Stress on Indo-Pak bilaterialsm on Kashmir and respect for the LOC in the context of the Kargil crisis if sustained could mark a significant turning point in the Chinese policy towards the Sub-continent.

Britain's Support: The Great Britain joined the United States in expressing strong support for the Indian position of Kargil. In a recent letter to the Prime Minister Mr. Atal Bihari Vajpayee, the British Premier Mr. Tony Blair commended India's restraint in Kargil.

Mr. Tony Blair, according to a spokesman of the Foreign office, is on record to say, "India's 'measured response' to Pakistan provocation had earned 'sympathy and support" from the international community. Mr. Blair said he had told Mr. Sharif that the Pakistan infiltration across the Line of Control had created a serious situation in Kargil.

United States of America: Mr. Bill Clinton, the American President, has played a very significant role in bringing the Pakistan to a reasonable stand by asking her to immediately withdraw from the Line of Control. It was there that the Pakistan Prime Minister declared that the intruders will withdraw from Kargil by 16th July, 1999. Having been isolated, feeling friendless, and pressurised from all quarters, Pakistan had no other option than to withdraw her regulars as well as the mercenaries from the Indian soil.

In one of its editorials, Hindu dated 18.6.1999, expressed the strong reaction of USA, against the Pakistani infiltration in the Kargil sector. I quote:

"At last a realisation must dawn on Pakistan of the international community's reaction to its infiltration across the line of control (LOC). In Kashmir in the past, the U.S. never came out so loud and clear against islamabad especially when India was involved. 'For once, Washington and the White House have been unambiguous, telling Mr. Nawaz Sharif to pull back his forces from across the LOC. Not only did the President Mr. Bill Clinton, convey this storng message to the Prime Minister, but the White House went public with his telephone conversation and its spokespersons were more than willing to speak to the Indian Media on what transpired. Pakistan no doubt feels let down, and the main opposition, Pakistan People's Party (PPP) seized on the opportunity to embarrass the government. In a very stringent statement the PPP decried the Sharif regime for its "foreign policy failure" and for the Pakistan being named intruder" by the international community. Rubbing salt to the government's wounds the party said Pakistan stood isolated because of the Kargil misadventure."

The G-8 Position on the Kargil Crisis

Here is a small interview given to Pioneer (carried in their issue dated July 11, 1999) by the French Ambassador to India, Claude Blanchemaison. And I quote:

Q: The G-8 position on Kargil became the subject of multiple interpretations. What really is the G-8 position on the issue?

A: The G-8 clearly stated that the intruders, whoever they are, must withdraw behind the Line of Control. India's external affairs Minister Jaswant Singh, who was in Paris on May 26, had the same kind of understanding from the French government. There is a lot of understanding for India in France which is consistent with the G-8 position.

Q: There have been reports that the G-8 communique was a backdoor attempt at pressing for greater international involvement in the Kashmir issue. Comments.

A: Our position has been consistent from the beginning, that Kashmir requires a bilateral solution between India and Pakistan as per the Simla Agreement.

Q: In the absence of a time frame given to Pakistan to withdraw from the LOC, for how long does the French in particular, and the G-8 in general, expect the Indian side to apply restraint on the LOC?

A: The Indian Prime Minister has been very wise in taking the position he has. The Indian armed forces are doing very well in clearing the Indian side of the LOC. There is no need for them to cross the LOC. Kargil hopefully will be finished soon. After Kargil, India has promised to resume the Lahore process. European countries are very happy about this statement.

Q: Your views on the current face-off between India and Pakistan in the context of a clearly unipolar world and its future ramifications on Asia.

A: The world has certainly changed. We are not living in a bipolar world anymore. Maybe we have not drawn all the consequences of the disappearance of bipolar world yet. Responsible countries are of course concerned about promoting peace and economic and social development. The situation in Asia should be seen through that angle now. In any case, India and France have a lot in common, especially the democratic political systems that the two share. Both of us also desire a multipolar world, which was made evident during President Jacques Chirac's visit to India last year.

That is the attitude we have taken in the recent period in which we have had some intense political dialogue with India on matters of economic interests and defence cooperation.

Russian Support for India: The Russian President, Boris Yeltsin took a principled stand at the G-8 Meet in Cologne, Germany, calling Pakistan to withdraw its militant infiltrators from the Indian Territory of Kashmir to immediately restore status quo ante along the line of control. Infact, Kargil was high on the agenda of the G-8, Annual Summit involving the USA, Britain, Canada, France, Germany, Japan, Italy and Russia.

According to a report published in Indian Express dated 20th June 1999, "This is the first time that a Kremlin Official has unequivocally called on the G-8, to lay the blame squarely on the door of Pakistan for the latest armed conflict in Kashmir."

In the past weeks almost all the member governments of the G-8 have individually recognised the unilateral violation of the LOC by Pakistan since the military action by Indian last month to flush out the militant intruders supported by Pakistan regulars from the Indian side of LOC. Russia has repeatedly accused Pakistan of provoking the situation by sending armed hands across the LOC.

Russia also asked Islamabad to "refrain from the violation of the conditions" of the well known agreements, demarcating the LOC, and warned that any attempt to change the LOC might lead to serious consequences.

NO INTELLIGENCE FAILURE

Almost all the opponent political parties have made up their mind to make Kargil crisis an Election Issue. Their main thrust is on the failure of the government, as to why they were not vigilant, and as to why they could not detect that the Pakistan had been sending the regulars and the mercenaries inside the Kargil sector. Leaving all other very vital issues concerning the welfare of the people at large, they have decided to focus the issue of intelligence failure on the part of the government, even at the cost of belittling the Jawans and their families. For this purpose, all these political parties have opened Kargil cells to pin down the government. Services of the expert advertising agencies are being taken to highlight the government failure on this aspect.

But here is a bad news for them who have decided to enter into this misadventure. Lt. General Krishan Pal in his latest interview to "Week" dated 8th August 1999 has set at rest the theory of "intelligence failure" in the Kargil crisis. According to the General, it was rather lack of advanced Surveillance system, than the intelligence failure. The General further observed that "he finds no reason to believe "that the intelligence failure facilitated Pakistan intrusion. In winter, image intelligence (satellite imagery) is difficult because of thick snow cover", he says. "But if there were forward looking thermal (infra-red) cameras, the heat differential could have picked up the intruders."

To a question, "Is manning the LOC the army's focus now?" The General replied, "It is physically not possible to cling on each rock. It has to be a combination of manpower and electronic surveillance. The process of establishing the state of the art surveillance has already started. It is not a matter of finance, but of identifying the right kind of equipment in a short time and trying it out in the extreme cold condition. When the General was asked, "What is the first step in preparing for winter deployment?", the General said, "We are already moving on with locating our troops at key points along the LOC. The basic equipment should be in place before the winter sets." Here are some more questions put to the General, to which he gave his reply.

Q: What was the key to success?

A: Team Work. Young officers led from the front, Commanding Officers climbed the peaks of the assault. The Brigade Commanders were in Tololing and point 5140 despite the age. No Brigade Commander was less than 52 years of age. Artillery did a great job.

Q: What problems would you face in deployment of troops in winter?

A: Main is logistics, elemental, the weather in these areas. Temperatures go down the minus 16 degrees and the snow accumulation is as much as 30 feet in some areas. We will need more snow mobiles. We will need all-terrain vehicles and more helicopter support

Q: Will the setting up of an inquiry Committee lead to a witch-hunt?

A: The panel will address various facets of war. We are very happy with it. It will focus on various shortcomings like the requirement of modern weapons and officer deficiency. I don't think they will look at the symptoms, but the real malaise.

Q: What about the failures,—intelligence, operation?

A: Failure is the inability to utilize available resources in an optimal fashion. Unless we know of the problems, the kind of equipment they had at their disposal it is not justified to make such sweeping statements. Our satellite and image intelligence give a resolution of six metres. With this you can't pick up a man or small camp.

Creating a fear psychosis of intelligence failure is not justified. Even in future do not expect miracles because we can't deploy resources required in the surveillance systems. The budget of modern armies for surveillance system is more than India's defence budget

And here are some questions put to the Defense Minister, to which he replied for this magazine.

Q: There have been attempts by Pakistan to capture features on LoC even as their troops were supposedly withdrawing.

A: As of this moment there are no Pakistani soldiers on our soil. They are in some areas on LOC and are being addressed where they are.

Q: The Army has demanded sophisticated surveillance equipment.

A: All the equipment that the Army, the air force and the navy are asking for are being procured post-haste.

Q: Will they be put in place before winter?

A: If there are items that may take longer time to be delivered, then one can't say so. But whatever is immediately required will be procured.

Q: Will you have problem with the Election Commission's Code of Conduct on releasing equipment to the army?

A: Not at all. How can anybody complain about equipping the army with the best available equipment.

Q: Will there be an increase in defence spending?

A: When our government came to office in March last year, we increased the defence budget by 11 per cent. The decline in the defence budget had begun a decade before that. We started setting it right. But a ten year gap cannot be made good in two years.

Q: How will extra resources for increased defence spending be generated?

A: The time has come for everyone to think where the money will come from. It is from the people—the tax payers. I hope every Indian will show the patriotic ferver that the Jawans displayed at the border. And I hope that those who are dodging tax over years, will prove their patriotism now by paying their taxes."

Panel on Kargil

The Government of India has already set-up a four member Committee, headed by K. Subrahmanyam, to review the events leading to Pakistan aggression in Kargil, and recommend measures to safeguard national security against such intrusions. The said Committee comprising Mr. K. Subramanyam, Lt. General (Retd.) K.K. Hazari, Mr. B.G. Verghese, and the National Security Council Secretary Mr. Satish Chandra. The Committee is expected to submit its report by 31st October, 1999.

The Committee, it is understood, has started its work in right earnest. Besides interacting with the armed forces and other government agencies and departments concerned, the Committee has invited inputs from the public based on reliable and authentic information. The government had already declared that the said Committee would have a comprehensive review of events that led to the Pakistan aggression. This decision was taken when the opposition demanded for a thorough probe into the Pakistani intrusion, alleging that there had been an intelligence failure.

According to George Fernandes, the Union Defence Minister, the army also had ordered internal inquiry into what went "wrong" which led to the intrusion. According to Pramod Mahajan the terms of reference of the Committee were wide enough and it was free to go into "anything and everything that may be political, administrative, or military failures."

In view of these two Committees set up for the sole purpose of finding out the truth about the aggression in Kargil, will it not be desirable for all the political parties, particularly those who wish to make Kargil an election issue, to come forward, and apprise the Committee of all the facts in their possession, so that the whole matter, which is of a very sensitive nature, comes to surface, and remedial measures are taken to avoid such intrusions in future. No heavens are going to fall if we wait for the report of Committee, which is going to submit its reports by 31st October, 1999. But if there only intention is to politicise the Kargil issue and humiliate, and disgrace the Jawan's blood in the political arena, simply to pin down the government during elections, then God alone can help them. The voters of our country are very wise, and mature, and are capable of sensing the designs of the political leaders, who are in the habit of playing different type of dirty and mean tactics during the elections.

The author as a humble citizen earnestly feels that the Kargil cells which have been opened by the political parties to belittle the Jawans for getting political mileage during the elections, should in all fairness, be converted into rehabilitation centres for the welfare of the Jawans and their families. Any criticism on the Kargil crisis which the political parties are hell bent to make, during elections should wait till the finding of the Committees, set up by the government and the Defence Ministry, are made public. Let us not prejudge the things.

FREE AND FAIR ELECTIONS
(Political Mudslinging—"Kargil")

Free and fair election is the hallmark of a democratic and representative government. India is one of the largest democratic countries of the world and has witnessed as many as 12 Lok Sabha elections. The change of government from time to time shows that the roots of democracy in our country are very deep and the voter of this country by and large is very mature and sensible and knows his duty very well. But this is not enough. Something more is the dire need of the hour. All the political parties, particularly the ruling party owe an onerous duty towards the country so that the democratic process works smoothly and peacefully. By entering into political mudslinging against each other, washing their dirty linen in public, criticising the government in power even at the cost of national security of the country and above all by putting candidates of shady character or with criminal background, they make the job of voter very difficult, in choosing the right type of person to represent his or her constituency. And the responsibility also lies on the shoulders of those who man the election process of the country, i.e., the Election Commission of India.

The Election Commission of India itself issued a Code of Conduct in 1984 after having a meeting with the representatives of all the political parties. The said Code of Conduct was designed to regulate the general conduct of political parties and candidates in the holding of election meetings, preventing the political parties from entering into political mudslingings, influencing the voters by unlawful means, entering into polling booths, and taking remedial measures in preventing all unlawful activities adopted by the political parties and their candidates.

People's Dilemma

People belonging to different schools of thought, particularly the non politicians (Doctors, Educationists, Journalists, Engineers, Industrialists, Lawyers, etc.) are in a great dilemma and are looking for a remedy which may give a stable government and good governance to the country. After the era of outside support, unholy alliances, raajneeti of joar-toar (politics of convenience), formation of coalition governments, criminalisation in politics and frequent dissolution of the Lok Sabhas prematurely, have become the order of the day and the foundation of all the democratic institutions have been shaken beyond repair. There has been a big question mark of the credibility of the institutions like, parliament, judiciary, bureaucracy, police etc. The Indian voter today is completely baffled, and is completely reduced to be a silent spectator. Inspite of the fact that he casts his vote to the best of his knowledge and full sense of responsiblilty, he stands betrayed by his own representative whom he sends to the Parliament or the Assembly. To his utter dismay, his elected representative keeps on changing colours for a quid pro-quo. It is here that something very seriously has got to be done, to bring drastic improvements in the present electoral system to bring stability and good governance in the country. The task is gigantic and not an easy one, but yet earnest efforts by all and sundry must continue. The time and space at our disposal are not adequate to discuss this problem elaborately in this small book, which is being brought out at such a short notice so as to reach every voter before the commencement of the election. But still we have made an earnest effort to give as much material as possible for the information and guidance of the voters who are in dire need, to act in the right direction at the 13th Lok Sabha Election

Justice G.T. Nanavati

The political situation has become so chaotic that even one of the judges of the Highest Court (Justice G.T. Nanavati) did not hesitate to express his views publicly in a seminar organised by senior lawyers at the India International Centre, the topic being—The Role of judiciary in Good Governance. To quote:

"Fifty years have passed since independence, but what have we achieved during this time? It can be said without hesitation that we do not have good governance even after such a long period. The state of affairs in the country has led to growing sense of frustration and despair. High expectations have given way to pessimism born out of misery, corruption, criminalisation and deterioration of moral values of life. The conduct of our elected representative of various legislative and governing bodies and the manner in which our executives exercise their power have shaken the very faith of the people in the institute of governance." Dr. Kashyap, who was associated with the parliament for over 37 years and served as the Secretary General of the Lok Sabha for some time, has very aptly described the situation: "Those in government are so pre-occupied with the struggle for survival in power that they have no time for addressing their attention to the problems of the people. There has been sharp erosion in the respect that people have for politicians. In many parts of the country, the government simply does not exist. Mafia gangs terrorise and rule, with the thin line fast disappearing between politicians and criminals."

Political Mudslinging and Kargil

Immediately after the elections to the Lok Sabha and the Legislative Assemblies have been announced by the election commission of India, the political parties, the ruling as well as the opponent parties, have started washing their dirty linen publicly to get as much political mileage as possible. But what is most disappointing and disturbing is, that all of them have made Kargil crisis, as their main issue. Whereas the ruling alliance is fully set up to cash the votes on their successful handling of situation in Kargil, the opponent parties have been over-enthusistically, preparing for pinning down the government, for their alleged intelligence failure on the Kargil crisis. The media has started highlighting the political agenda of all the political parties maligning each other, making Kargil the main election issue. Here is a sample of some highlights of the verbal bouts between the Congress Party and the BJP.

Congress Speaking Sharif Language: BJP

The Bhartiya Janata Party has charged congress for speaking the language of Pakistani Prime Minister Nawaz Sharif. When the entire world is questioning Pakistan for its misadventure in Kargil, the Congress is bent on posing question to the Indian Government.

The BJP has decided to give a befitting reply to the campaign unleashed by the Congress. The Congress has decided to ask one question per day to the BJP on Kargil. In a counter attack for every question raised by the Congress the BJP is going to highlight government achievements. As Mr. Naidu stated, "We will highlight one achievement of Vajpayee government everyday".

Condemning the congress indulgence in politics of negativism, the BJP said its desperation is evident from the fact that its leader has become de facto non option as a Prime Ministerial candidate; its party has been jolted by a major split; it is virtually issueless on any ideological issue and potential allies are discredited lot.

As Mr. Naidu pointed out, "With allies such as Laloo and Ms. Jayalalitha all it has in common is the corrupt image of the Congress and its allies."

If the Prime Minister Mr. Atal Bihari Vajpayee could shake hand in Lahore, he also had the courage to crush the neighbours for indulging in misadventure in Kargil. And when the world stood by India, the Congress continues to strike a discordant note.

The BJP spokesperson recalled that from the very beginning the Congress has worked against the national interest. As Mr. Naidu said, "when the nation stood by the army, the Congress issued a statement a day inquiring into the alleged

Intelligence Failure." Again when the G-8 issued a statement pointing to Pakistan as the guilty party launching a pad for world support to India, the Congress reacted to the contrary. Pakistan holds India accountable for Kargil and Congress holds Mr. Vajpayee accountable for Kargil.

Congress Poses Questions to BJP: In a move aimed at embarrassing the Government on Kargil Issue, Congress on tuesday began posing a series of questions on the conflict and asked the government as to when it first came to know of the infiltration and who, in Prime Minister's view, was responsible for failure.

In the first set of questions released by party spokesman Ajit Jogi, the Congress said the nation had a right to know as to when the Prime Minister personally learnt of Pakistani violations of the LOC and in his view who was responsible for failure. "He himself? His government? or some other minister?"

Jogi suggested that answers to these queries was important as the Prime Minister himself had been compelled to confess to the failure of vigilance on the country's frontiers.

(Pioneer—14.7.1999)

Congress Campaign to Blast BJP on Kargil

The die is cast. The Congress will be taking on the BJP straight on the Kargil intrusions in the Lok Sabha elections with its ad campaigns challenging the adversary primarily on security front.

The party has finalised the advertising agencies and they have been briefed to conjure up a campaign that targets the BJP on its failures on various fronts, specially on the inability to defend the borders at Kargil. Besides Madhyam, which has handled earlier campaigns of the party, the list includes Mumbai-based Madison owned by Sam Balsara, Livewire from Hydrabad, concept form Delhi and Sony from Calcutta.

Selected out of two dozen agencies vying for the Congress election account, the five have been asked to prepare presentations by this weekend by the party's campaign committee headed by Pranab Mukherjee. Apart from the three Bs of the BJP—Bomb, Budget and Bus—the Congress campaign will be lampooning it with Bigotry and Betrayal

(Economic Times—27.7.1999)

Steady Old Hand

It is a battle time and India's grand old party is on the warpath. Pegged back by the flare-up in Kargil, the Congress is all set to embark on an aggressive campaign to wrest back the initiative. The party has carefully fashioned a two-pronged strategy. Its immediate objective is to puncture the ruling coalition's halo of the Kargil war and expose misadventures like the Lahore Bus ride and the Nuclear tests. The long-term goal is to protect itself as the only party capable of providing a stable government.

The Congress plans to checkmate the BJP's attempt to appropriate the nationalistic high grounds by differentiating between the army's achievements and the government's failure. Congress President Sonia Gandhi has begun to hammer home the point that the intrusions were inflicted on the nation because the government lowered its guard. "If the government had reacted in time, our brave Jawans would not have had to lay down their lives", she said at a public meeting in Madhya Pradesh.

The party has also been stressing the fact that it was the armed forces who ultimately saved the day. "The crown of glory belongs to the forces and not Vajpayee," says the party's spin doctor Kapil Sibal. The special Kargil cell of the Congress—headed by cwc member Pranab Mukherjee and comprising K. Natwar Singh, Sibal and Mani Shankar Aiyar—has been meeting daily sometimes even twice a day to calibrate the party's response. "We have accepted the BJP's challenge and will take the issue from village to village," says cwc member Rajesh Pilot.

(India Today—9.8.1999)

It looks all the political parties are going to waste crores of rupees in successfully maligning each other, making Kargil as the main election issue. Will it not be advisable for all of them to spend that huge amount for the welfare of the jawans and their families, who are in dire need of financial assistance at that moment. I hope good sense will prevail on all those who have ventured to enter this misadventure.

In the end, I reproduce below what a great son of the soil, T.N. Seshan, former dynamic Chief Election Commissioner had said as a piece of advice to all and sundry, while the jawans were fighting at Kargil.

All of us Must Speak in One Voice: T.N. Seshan

"The job on hand is to get the infiltrators and the Pakistani soldiers out. And our soldiers and airmen are facing tremendous odds in doing this. The Pakistani infiltrators are sitting on the peaks over the Srinagar-Leh highway. And they are in an advantageous position. At the moment, all that the country should do is not to speak in a distorted voice but support the men in the field.

The deaths of our soldiers and airmen are tragic losses irrespective of whether they are colonels or sepoys. These are not mere statistics. To individuals and families, they are terrible personal calamitites. We must remember this and support them in their darkest hour.

War is a terrible affair at all times. And one wishes that Pakistan does not resort to it. Without entering into any polaric discussions, I want to say that Pakistan has once again proved that they are unreliable; no, even more than that, they are hostile and deceitful neighbours.

Pakistan was born in hatred. And so long as you have a quarrelsome neighbour, that quarrel will erupt at some point or the other. For the moment I merely want to say that eternal vigilance is the price of liberty. If we are not vigilant, somebody or the other will take advantage of us.

It is a matter of tremendous satisfaction that the large masses of people realise that this is the time to stand united, though some discordant voices have been raised by politicians here and there. Those who are eternally suffering from the disease of verbal diarrhea must take steps to prevent that diarrhea from causing national damage."

(As told to K.R. Sreenivas)
(Indian Express—12.6.1999)

L' AFFAIRE KARGIL

UNESCO's catch-word is 'war starts, in the mind'. The opening of battle front in Kargil and harping on more Kargils indicates the mind-set of Pakistan. According to Teesta Setalvad, Pakistan, resolve to complete the "unfinished agenda of Partition", despite the fact that two-nation theory has been seriously challenged within Pakistan. And what is being pursued with single-minded devotion is not just a territorial proxy war, but also an attempt to impose the highly regimental Wahabi Islam on a valley renowned for its Rishism (Sufism).

Former Vice-Chief of Army staff M.L. Thapar states, that militarily, we had the upper hand in driving out the Pakistan's raiders from Kashmir in 1948, they were on the run when the matter was unilaterly referred to UN and cease fire was declared. An opportunity to settle the issue, once and for all time, was lost.

Uneasy stalemate ensued till 1965, when a massive infiltration called "Operation Gibralter was launched by Pakistan in Kashmir. Our military response both in Kashmir and Punjab resulted in capturing strategic territory—Haji Pir pass in Kashmir and substantial advance in Sialkat and Lahore, but this was set at naught after the Tashkent agreement, when a status quo ante was restored. 1972 is a tragic milestone on the long inept handling of Kashmir. We then had not only captured territory but also returned more than 90,000 Pakistani Prisoners of war to a bargaining counters for Pakistan to be compelled to agree to recognise the line of actual control as being the international boundary of the factual decision of Kashmir. One does not know, what the compulsions of Indian Prime Minister were for not to draft an agreement which would have clinched the Kashmir issue irrevocably. A golden opportunity was deliberately cast away.

Colonel (Retd.) S.R. Nanda, had given a detailed account of intelligence failures from 1947 to 1962. The main thrust of Nanda in his article, "Intelligence failure" is on the structure of the intelligence agencies. Major weakness of our intelligence agencies is that from the Director downward these are all packed with police cadre as was the case during British Raj. Our intelligence miserably failed in 1958, when the Chinese occupied the Aksai Chin area during 1962 & 1965 wars against China and Pakistan respectively. The crucial letter of 7 November, 1950 of Sardar Patel to Nehru about the security of borders with China was ignored at political level.

First time the President of India advised the functioning government to seek for a vote of confidence. The grand secular front pulled down the government and staked a claim with imaginary total of 272 MP's supposed to be ready to supplant the Vajpayee government in five minutes.

People to people contact was initiated by Vajpayee at Lahore, but as usual Pakistan did not like the sane idea and stealthily captured area of Mushkov, Dras, Kargil and Batalik sectors and threated Srinagar-Leh Road.

The undeclared battle was met militarily with air force and the operation Vijay was launched. The battle was won, all the infiltrators were evicted, posts recaptured and this time no territory was surrendered. Diplomatically, Kargil was the first battle in which the international community realised the true motives of Pakistan and backed India's Herculian restraint. The battle was fought at high altitude. Acclimatisation is essential at the heights of 10,000 ft and above. This takes a minimum of 10 days when troops are moved in stages to higher altitude upto 17,000 ft before being inducted into action. All equipment, ammunition and supplies have to be carried manually at these heights as no other form of transport are available.

The Congress pushed the country to uncalled for election, cut the life of the functioning elected government from the 5 years to 13 months. Encouraged by these developments, Pakistan betrayed the trust reposed militarily for not occupying the post beyond the line of control. Openly Pakistan does not own the part of its military in this battle. The dead military personnel were buried by Indian army as Pakistan has no cheek to betray the military code being followed by more than 27 years in these high altitudes.

The political parties are hungry for issues for going to people in these "thrust" elections on the people. The real issues of Health, Education, Stability, Law and order etc. seem to have been shelved by political parties. And it is in the winds that Kargil is going to be the election plank.

The following propositions are current:

1. Kargil battle was won.
2. Government is responsible for intelligence failure, it is victory for Jawans & not for government.
3. Kargil should not be made election issue.

Soumitro Das opined that there is no point in saying it is victory for the Jawans and not for government. The wave of patriotic fervour although focussed on the Army's Valour in the face of grim odds, understandably went to the government. There is not much the Congress can do about it, not even by raising question, which in current mood, appear to be mere hairsplitting. Finally, the saying that the BJP was responsible for "murdering" soldiers in Kargil is an awful *faux pas,* goes dead against the rhetoric of patriotism, national pride and sacrifice, which will play for long time.

In fact, the best way for the BJP to exploit the Kargil conflict for electoral purposes is to let the congress go hammer and tongs against Vajpayee and dig up all errors of omissions that have led to situation in the first place. This will reveal the omissions of the Congress vis-a-vis the other parties and clarify the position for all to know.

Just released Encarta World English Dictionary by Microsoft Corporation has a Microspeak "offline", meaning to remove something such as a discussion from a public forum to a private one.

Kargil issue should not be made the election plank, so to say "offline" it is not based on sane thinking. It is the prerogative of the people for discussion of Kargil Syndrome, raising its ugly head very often. Election time is the only time when the people come face to face with their leaders. After election the elected persons become touch-me-not commodity. There are security and bureaucratic iron walls between the voter and the elected persons. People of India are brave and can not be mislead by politically hairsplitting the Kargil issue. The Indian People echoed with one voice the couplet of urdu poet "Anis", about the relation of Kashmir with them:

Mera Bharat Too Dil May Rehta Hai,
Dil Mera Kargil May Rehta Hai,
Umar Usko Hamari Lag Jaye,
Jo Batalik Ki Hill May Rehta Hai

(My India is in my heart. My heart is in Kargil. We sacrifice our life for him who live in Batalik hill.)

Kewal Krishan Sharma*

* Advocate, Supreme Court of India, New Delhi.

FREE DEBATE ON KARGIL

Cacophony of delirious exultation orchestrated over Pokharan II and Kargil 'Triumph' (if at all it was a triumph) by some segments of Public manifests sheer Jinogism and has in fact obfuscated the real issues. If any sane voice is raised questioning the rationale behind nucrealisation and Sabre-rattling on the Soil of Gandhi, it is dubbed as an unpatriotic act. Some genuinely feel that if there had been no Pokharan there would not have been Kargil and it is we who bestowed nuclear parity on Pakistan which encouraged them to have eye-ball to eye-ball contact. Militarily ten times stronger than Pakistan, as we claim to be, could not otherwise have the guts to take on us. In the past we smashed them several times.

In democracy, the affairs of the state ought to be run by an elected government who according to constitutional norms is supposed to be accountable to the people through the instrumentality of Parliament, but when there is no lok sabha the lame duck government for the interregnum should act like a guardian and a trustee of judiciary waiting to gain majority. The caretaker government is like a night watchman. But if such nightman becomes arrogant and commits malfeasaner and unsavoury acts the very confidence in the concept of guardship is eroded. I am not afraid to say that the caretaker government has not acted an honest guardian. They have arrogant to themselves such draconian powers which would not otherwise be wielded and exercised by a responsible elected government. Even a despot would not behave as they have done. They have surcharged the atmosphere with hysterical utterances, aggressive and arrogant behaviour which tend to impinge upon objective debate.

Maturity of democracy can be measured from the standard of public debate on important public issue concerning the nation. In the vibrating and pulsating democracy transparency and accountability are hallmarks. Negation of debate militants against the very concept of democratic liberism. Debate on Kargil should not at all be impugned, constricted or restricted or straijackled in any manner. Despite demand for Rajya Sabha session made by the opposition duly endorsed by the President of India has been denied on very specious, incognet and unconvincing reasons. The present junta of rules appear to have run amuck and acquired draconian propensities and has shown profanes disrepect to the sentiments of people and the head of the realm. People are eager to know the genesis of Kargil imbroglio. By denying debate suspicion in the mind of people is bound to get reinforced that they have something damaging to them to hide.

Countdown has commenced and in couple of weaks from now we will be going to hustings, Election time is the time to seek rendition of account from the legislative representatives. It is said by some intellectual and observers that Kargil should not be made an election issue by the political parties. May it be, yet nothing can stop the people from raising the issue of Kargil particularly those who have received body-bags. Sooner or later these questions will be begging answers:

1. Why we allowed intrusion?
2. What was the role of intelligence agencies?
3. What action has been taken against the delinquent intelligence personal?
4. Was there lack of political will to combat the intrusion in time?
5. Could Kargil be avoided if there had been proper vigilance?
6. What steps are proposed to be taken to avoid replay of Kargil? and so on and so forth.

Whatever the reasons were there, intrusion took place and our defence forces have classical the Kargil and other areas from intrusion. The Defence personnel as dictated by discipline will never question as to why such a situation was allowed to obtain where they without adequate equipment had to lay their lives. Folly of rulers often has to be borne by defense personnel. It is for the people to quiz as to why the defense personnel were thronged into deadly peril. Our brothers and sones who have opted for defense services are not cannon fodder. They are most pariotic and in the event of emergency they would not hesitate to shed blood for the mother land. But primarily it is the duty of the leadership to ensure that war should not be thrust upon our men unnecessarily. Our martyrdomlogy is very rich, we need not wage war to create martyrs. There are other fields also where our people can show chivallary and gallantry.

In Art of War Su Tzu Wu said:
Place your Army in deadly peril,
and it will survive, plunge it into
desperate straits and it will come off
in safely."

Kargil is over. Let us not rejoice on that. It is time for nation to do introspection, take measures to avoid repetition of Kargil and show solidarity with the victims of Kargil. Let us develop such mechanism to ensure that there is no war.

Avtar Singh Sohal*

* Advocate, Supreme Court of India, New Delhi.

DIVERSITY IN UNITY
Backfire, the Kargil Issue

Democracy is not a way of governing, but primarily a way of determining who shall govern and, broadly to what ends.

The 12th Lok Sabha passed into history to give birth to 13th Lok Sabha-'Kargil is the issue'. There is lull. Guns are silent and the intruders have been shown the exit across the LOC. But Kargil is still hot-shot to the election. Kargil to be Congress main poll plank, says Sonia. BJP to take on Congress on Kargil issue. So is the case with other Political setups. Spare Army from Politics: Gen. Malik. A mad race to cash on the carcass of the soldiers who fought the odds with the odds and laid their life for the cause of the country with motto 'Service before self'-a paradigm for our politicians.

Kargil is an issue of lessons and not an issue of Election. It is time to introspection and not for witch-hunting. Our soldiers succeed. Where do we fail? Indian democracy is sailing through the troubled water. Authoritarianism and its resultant anarchy has fast engulfed all other perimeters. The prime minister, Atal Bihari Vajpayee after losing confidence motion in parliament stated, "Democracy in India, appears to have become a hollow shell", with election, "reduced to a farce".

Country and the people demand socio-politico-economic radical reforms, who will fulfill these aspirations?

Ride the ass that carries rather than a horse that throws.

Y.P. Singh*

* Advocate, Supreme Court of India, New Delhi.

SPOILERS AND SAVIOURS OF KARGIL

Kargils are a must to realise that survival is only for the fittest. Nations born without a blood-bath need more Kargils to ensure and preserve the strength that lies in unity. Every single family thereby would learn to sacrifice, whether high or low, to make the deed, of our soldiers in uniform, meaningful. There could be no other way to win a Kargil, because in the ultimate analysis there is no other way to bring peace in the wake of misery and destruction inflicted in terms of cost and human lives lost. Will it be more meaningful to have utilised these very resources to avert, avoid or delay Kargils? Can we find a solution to this issue through pre-election debates?

It is the pride in you that represents the nation in uniform. Kargil is therefore another symbol of pride resulting therefrom. We could therefore debate Kargil before it becomes the bone of contention in the streets. Such Kargils had flashed a number of times during the last 50 years of our nationhood. But lessons learnt from such Kargils were forgotten sooner than soon, because of weak opposition of the ruling party in power. This trend therefore over a long period of governance dulls the impact on the nation, which turns complacent and its ability to guard off Kargils gets diluted.

The Kargil of 1999 has clearly demonstrated that it's the leadership both at political level and fighting forces domain, which it allowed to come into play in responsible manner at the opportune times, could pay hefty dividends in terms of victories all round. Kargil today is therefore a very important and a meaningful issue to be debated upon in the parliament and not in the streets with slogans, and aptly it is for the insensitive politicians who thereby could take others for a ride, knowing too well that Kargils do get repeated unless these Kargils are treated with respect at all times, and not necessarily at the election time.

We should therefore select the election manifestos without involving Kargil, and try to bring out what interests the people otherwise, to help the parties to win more seats in the ensuing election. It would be a great service to the nation if all the parties at least agree to shelve the Kargil related issues, till the elections are over, and then wait for the right forum and opportunity in the parliament, to predict and prepare for the next Kargil without hiding behind the past failures of the half a century gone by with neglect of defence.

Brig. Mohindra Singh Gill (Retd.)*

* Advocate, Supreme Court of India, New Delhi.

SO, WHO'S BELITTLING THE TROOPS

For the BJP and Congress, Our soldier's Blood is Merely a Political Tool, Says Sumir Lal

The Sheer Brazenness took one's breath away. There is the icy heights of Kargil, our soldiers are dying in number that should shame us, paying with their lives for intelligence failures, administrative incompetence and complacent policy-making. Here, in the comfortable plains, we are being told not to cross-examine the government, the minister, the past, the future, because we must all stand together lest we demoralise the troops. Don't politicise the conflict, post mortems must wait. Being good citizens, we agree.

But when we opened our newspapers on Wednesday, what did we see? We saw an advertisement which said, "More than a hundred of our soldiers have laid down their lives in the battle for Kargil". The names of some of them were printed and, below, was the BJP lotus. In a corner, in the humblest print possible, was the apologetic line, "Issued by Bharatiya Janata Party." How wonderful, we thought, the ruling party paying such touching homage to the martyrs.

Then we turned the page. And what did we see? An identical ad in an identical slot. Continuing from the previous one, it said, "The first one did so in 1953". It was referring to Shyama Prasad Mookerjee, founder of the BJP's forerunner, the Jana Sangh, who had died in person after courting arrest during a demonstration on Kashmir. The copy below read: "At Kargil hundreds of our valiant soldiers have made the supreme sacrifice. The nation must remember, the BJP led government is determined to drive out the enemy from Indian soil. The government is run by those who have, more than anybody else, shown exemplary commitment to the cause". The lotus, this time, proudly stood on the legend "Bharatiya Janata Party".

In one cynical, emotion-exploiting moment, the BJP's media managers had equated the bloody, idealistic heroism of Sqn-Ldr Rajiv Ahuja, Maj. Mariappan Saravana. Capt. Amol Kalia and their brave colleagues with the coincidental death in prison of their party's founder. And used those seconds before the newspaper reader could recover his poise to associate their party alone with the courageous efforts of the armed forces. If this is not politicisation, if this is not belittling the sacrifices of the soldiers, if this is not exploiting the patriotic sentiments aroused by the conflict for narrow political gain, I wonder what is. If I were the Army Chief, I would protest most vehemently to the Prime Minister.

Why haven't the BHP's opponents reacted to this audacious attempt to gain electoral mileage out of a (party self-created) national crisis and, in hundreds of homes, a personal tragedy? The Congress spokesman did make a muted protest, but he lacked conviction, didn't he?

For, the previous day, one of his own partymen has placed an advertisement. This worthy, going by the name of Ramesh Handa, used a stirring graphic of three silhouetted soldiers atop a hill unfurling the Tricolour, with a poem in Hindi alongside extolling the sacrifices of the Mother's brave sons. No prizes for guessing who the "Mother" is: Sonia Gandhi, of course, smiling with folded hands from one corner of the ad.

The Congress' only defence can be that, unlike the BJP, the party has not officially issued that ad. It is clearly the work of an over-enthusiastic sycophant, and nowhere does the name of the party of its electoral symbol figure. But that is just a quibble, for the association is unmistakable. If the Congress' motives were pure, it should have immediately disowned this ad and even threatened Handa with disciplinary action. Indeed, the reprimand should have come from Sonia Gandhi herself, for the ad clearly attempts to identify her with the upsurge in patriotic sentiment.

So there you have it. The BJP in its typical planned, cold-blooded manner, and the Congress in its characteristic anarchic style have attempted to exploit the blood of our fighting men, and the sentiment its spilling has aroused in us, to derive partisan advantage. Their culpability is compounded because they happen to be the ruling party and main opposition. What makes it all the more galling is that, between them, they have contributed the most historically and currently to the present crisis.

One can be certain that this is just the beginning, for the electoral campaign will only get increasingly intense, bitter and unscrupulous over the next three months as the polls approach. If the military top brass, lay citizenry and more sensible elements in the political leadership do not take a stand now, the BJP's Machiavellis and Congress' Marie Antoinettes will have completely politicised and trivialised the heroism of the men in Kargil by the time of the elections. This, in turn, will have bred in the public an insensitivity about the military, and played complete havoc with troop morale. Are we sacrificing our lives for the motherland or to help the BJP and Congress, the boys will wonder, and lower their resolve.

The Prime Minister and his Cabinet colleagues come across as most hypocritical, therefore, when they invoke notions like "troop morale" and need for "unity" to fend off legitimate questions about the sequence of events that led to the Kargil intrusion, and to avoid debate on their security, foreign policy and military strategies.

Such concerns, we now know, do not apply to them in their quest for votes. But they are convenient covers to fling at anyone in the media or intelligentsia who asks anything uncomfortable. But since the BJP-Congress, through these ads, have revealed just how deep their concern for the soldiers' welfare actually is, perhaps it is time the rest of us cast aside the traps of "national duty" and "responsibility" to ask. Would it really demoralise the troops if mistakes and strategies are discussed and critiqued in a balanced, informed and non-partisan manner?

It is in the interest of the government and military top brass to suppress such examination, for it could result in some red faces. But my instinct is that the men and officers of the battlefront will welcome it if the nation acknowledges, and then rectifies, the blunders for which they are paying, and if the government's diplomatic and military options are thoroughly examined. The troops can only benefit if the country honestly addresses the difficulties and self-inflicted handicaps (such as those related to equipment) they are facing. We need an "ante mortem" rather than post mortem, so that corrections can be made even as the situation unfolds.

Is it unpatriotic and irresponsible to raise these questions now? The ruling party has no right to answer as, after last week's shameless ads, it has done the worst damage itself by converting our soldiers' blood into a political tool.

Courtesy: Hindustan Times, 27 June, 1999

THE INEVITABLE POLITICISATION OF KARGIL

One of the more native, indeed laughable, propositions to have emerged from the ongoing war in Kargil is that the crisis should not be "politicised". This stems from a generally accepted belief that a war is something so sacrosanct that if should not fall victim to as vulgar a practice as politics and that political parties should refrain from exploiting the events on the borders for their own, partisan and narrow ends.

Nothing could be more absurd. For starters, there is nothing, not culture, nor sport and certainly and defence, which is outside the ambit of politics and to expect that a political parties will, or should eschew such subjects is to live in cloud cuckoo land. The entire country may be one in wanting to throw out the Pakistani intruders and many political parties may not want to raise needlessly divisive questions about the situation a this juncture, but they will assess the war, its prelude and its aftermath, in a political light. That is what politics is all about.

Secondly, one cannot forget that the war has come just before the country will go to polls for the third time in three years. These are elections everyone claims no one wanted and have been allegedly foisted on the country. But they are a fact of life and everyone is fervently hoping that this time at least the electorate will provide a result which will bring about the all-elusive stability the country needs. Convincing the voter that one party is more equipped to provide that stability is the task of all political parties and alliances and for this they need an issue; what better issue than a war, which can demonstrate decisiveness and confidence and which touches an emotional chord of the people?

Ever since 1977, when the Janata Party rode to power and portrayed itself as the saviour of democracy before the people, generally elections in India have been centred around one key issue. In 1984, the country was worried about the aftermath of Mrs. Indira Gandhi's brutal assassination and there were fears of the country breaking up. Five years later, Rajiv Gandhi had to face the fusillade of the Bofors gun and Swiss accounts with exotic names, which the opposition exploited to the hilt. Mandal and Mandir followed and the Congress returned to power after the second phase of elections after Rajiv Gandhi's assassination.

In 1998, the Bharatiya Janata Party had managed to convince people that it would provide an able and stable government, something that the people yearned for after two Third Front government (and the BJP's own 13-day wonder) collapsed prematurely. But after their one year performance in power, which is for everyone to see, the BJP could not have possibly played the "government with a difference" card; a party which cannot keep its allies within the fold cannot claim to offer stability. A campaign based on Sonia Gandhi's ethnic origins could work up to a point and would have tapped into the urban fence-sitters' natural ambivalence about foreigners, but an overkill could have proved counter-productive, as Bal Thackeray discovered during the Assembly elections last year.

The Congress too would have been on Shaky ground if it had tried to play up "stability " as a strength, especially since it too was losing important leaders because of the stranglehold of the dynasty. This therefore would have been and issueless election which may have thrown up a Lok Sabha no different from the previous one.

Kargil provides the ideal political debating point. Traditionally, governments in power derive maximum benefit from wars (as Mrs. Margaret Thatcher can testify) and a decisive victory can yield lucrative electoral victories. Though the 1971 general election took place before and not after the Bangladesh war and surrender in December, the next year's Assembly elections saw Indira Gandhi's Congress put up a spectacular performance. Hence, it is almost certain that the BJP and its allies will reap the fruits of the Indian Army's performance, which would have been the same whoever had been at the helm of affairs.

Having grasped that simple fact, the BJP has incorporated the spirit of Kargil in its election plans—the somewhat tasteless (and factually incorrect) party ads appropriating all the martyrdom of Indian soldiers, the effective drumming up of a nationalist sentiment all over the country, the use of the government media to evoke patriotism with all the requisite films and music (one martial documentary even played Wagner's Ride of the Valkyries in the background!), all point to a sustained campaign to build a mood of intense patriotism which can only work to the advantage of the incumbent Government. A successful transition has been made from being a caretaker government to being a caring government, as a DAVP ad so cleverly put it. How does this sit with the repeated exhortations of BJP leaders that the war should not be politicised?

The other parties, notably the Congress but also the Left, have been caught squarely on the backfoot. The Congress is still assessing how to approach the issue and its measured analysis of the diplomatic implications of the war are not likely to be heard over the din of victory drums. In addition, if the party is honest enough to admit it, it knows that it will have to contend with the explosive cocktail of gung-ho patriotism and doubts about a person of foreign origin leading the country; not surprisingly the connection has already been established by the other anti-Congress parties.

To be sure, the party, like the Left and other anti-BJP parties, are keeping the powder dry and will definitely raise questioning once the war is over and the election campaign starts in real earnest. The global diplomatic pressures on India that are sure to follow, the high price paid in human terms and the fact of the intrusion itself: The many questions about Kargil in the aftermath are not limited to those who are necessarily against the parties in power and these will have to be answered. It will be extremely surprising if the Congress and the Left do not pick up these issues, which are bound to have a resonance in semi-urban and rural areas and perhaps even in sections of the urban middle-class. Where one section celebrates the martyrdoms of a soldier in defence of the motherland, his family might worry about the loss of a bread-winner.

Exploiting the successes and valour of the Indian Armed forces therefore will not be a zero-sum equation. As a political tactic it will have to be handled sensitively or it could prove counter-productive. The spontaneous burst of solidarity and patriotism by Indians will turn to disgust if the sacrifices of Indian soldiers are seen as just another pawn in a cynical and narrow political game. Already there are misgivings over the burst of corporate enthusiasm to wave the flag and at the stridency of parties like the Shiv Sena which are pursuing their own nefarious agendas. Nor are the people fully convinced that the victory in Kargil belongs to any one party and an attempt to hijack it could boomerang.

In any event, it remains to be seen if the voter will see Kargil quite the same way as the politicians and if the constituency beyond the middle-classes will feel quite so jingoistic about the war. In the end, this war too may not be able to create a big swing which the two big parties so desperately need—at best it could help consolidate the existing positions. It is this realisation, more than the self-righteousness being displayed by all and sundry, which may in the end prevent the Kargil victory from becoming totally "politicised".

Courtesy: Sidharth Bhatia in Pioneer, July 13, 1999

AFTER THE KARGIL CUP FEVER

"Please Tell the Government from all the mothers that we do not want martyr status and publicity. We want those who are responsible for bringing the intruders into the country to be punished," lamented one of the parents of Captain Anuj Nayyar, as the family waited for the body of their brave son who died in the battlefield.

Only the Statesman reporter deemed it worthwhile to record the anguish of the Nayyar family. When on Sunday, July 11, Captain Nayyar was cremated with full military honours, the reporter was doggedly at hand to record the pain of another family member: "What value are their (politicians') was condolences five days after our nephew was killed in a futile situation, which should never developed in the first place? How did the 'intruder' enter our country at all?"

The reporter, who recorded the Nayyars' discordant not in the triumphal celebration of the Kargil-induced feel-good nationalism, is liable to be accused of professional solecism; after all, the herd-leaders—both in the print and electronic media—had spotted the potency of martyrdom as a gripping story. Kargil was too good a story to be dealt with routinely. The country had to be fed with graphic depictions of the booming gun.; the macho spirit had to be pampered; and, the kleig lights must be turned on the dead soldiers' relations who are made to utter the syrupy poetry of martyrdom. For the professional vendors of news, Kargil turned out to be just as good a story as was the World Cup a couple of months ago. The same feverish energy was brought to bear on the coverage of the "Kargil cup" as was displayed during the World Cup. Except that there was no corporate sponsorship of the Kargil war, the parallels between the two events were depressingly chilling. There was the same mass cranking up on emotions; correspondents/cameramen were rushed to the arena to produce cover stories, as was done during the World Cup; and, just as during the cricket season, retired captains and players were resurrected to chatter endlessly to the Harsha Bhogles and studio anchorpersons, retired soldiers and strategists were cajoled to come to television studios to expound on the latest development from the war-front.

A mock but furious debate was conducted on whether or not the Indian Army should cross the Line of Control; not very different from the one on Azharuddin's suitability as captain. Before the Indian team left for England, hefty cash awards were announced for the players should they come back with the Cup; now the State Governments and individual politicians and vying with one another on announce awards for the families of the Kargil heroes. The process of packaging "Kargil" has not been very different from the marketing of the World Cup. And, think of it, all this without the intervention of the spinmeisters, who must be marvelling at the susceptibilities of the professional story-tellers in the media.

Granted, Kargil was not all fun and game; and, granted, that a very large number of young men had to pay with their lives for the foolishness of the political masters in Delhi, the question is: how long will the "Kargil fever" last, and whether it would overwhelm the electorate to such an extent that the voter will forget the basic issues of (mis) governance that were so palpable visible before the ISI cabal decided on its little adventure in Kargil? It is quite possible that the television-induced Kargil fever would also recede as did the ephemeral World Cup frenzy; but it is more probable that the BJP partisans, the Sangh Parivar propagandists, the corporate crooks and the Sonia-must-be-stopped-at-all-costs polemicists would join hands to keep the Kargil flame burning bright. No model code of conduct can prevent this or that governmental department from buying newspaper space or television spots to pay homage to the Brave Soldier. The post-Kargil nationalistic emotionalism will be cashed in on unabashedly. Mr. L.K. Advani's four Bs—Bomb, Bus, Bihar and Budget—would be forgotten and will give way to three Ws—Washington, War and War Widows.

In other words, what the Indian polity is likely to see is perhaps the most successful ISI intervention in our internal affairs, so much so that its actions have more or less set the agenda for the coming polls. The Parliamentary Affairs Minister, Mr. P.R. Kumaramangalam, has already made bold to assert that under the Kargil-tested able leadership of Mr. Atal Behari Vajpayee, the BJP-led National Democratic Alliance would garner more than 300 Lok Sabha seats; the Minister is entitled to his wild optimism, but he must be thankful to the ISI strategists in Islamabad for this turn of events, if at all things turn out the ruling combine's way. A political party that has all these years railed against the omnipresent ISI is now praying to reap the benefits of the ISI stupidities (though even after 14 months at the Home Ministry, Mr. L.K. Advani could not produce the much-promised White Paper on the Pakistani agency.)'

Admittedly, the Indian voter's mood is notoriously fickle; he is prone to change his mind every six weeks, and it is quite possible that by the time he starts queuing up outside the polling booths on September 4, the collective mood will have moved beyond the post-Kargil emotion-moved beyond the post-Kargil emotionalism. And, that exactly is the challenge before the polity and its operators: how to convert the elections into a massive popular audit on the acts of omission and commission of the BJP-led Government at the Centre.

By definition, a general election is an opportunity for the electorate to pass a judgment on whether it approved of the performance of the incumbent government. The ruling party of parties have a legitimate right to put a gloss on their achievements and failures, and to impress upon the voter that they deserve another stint at office to carry on their good work similar, the Opposition groups and individuals have the democratic privilege of pointing out the inadequacies of the Government and to convince the voter that their alternative policies, programmes and personalities deserve a chance. Therefore, the Indian polity would definitely find itself short-changed if the artificial and temporary Kargil fever influences the voter's choice over the design and content of the governing arrangement in New Delhi over the next five years.

To the extent the BJP takes considerable pride in asserting that it has provided the first genuine non-Congress Government at the Centre, it is all the more reason for the ruling party to summon up the courage of its propaganda to want to educate the voter on the correctness of the Vajpayee Government's track record. Before the Kargil conflict, the BJP leadership had opted to advertise the genuineness of its non-Congress credentials in Pokhran, Orissa, the Dangs and in Dr. Murli Manohar Joshi's Ministry, where an attempt was made to saffronise the textbooks. The Congress(I) and other political parties owe it to themselves and to the country to slice, dice and dissect for the voter's benefit the BJP's pre-Kargil essay in sectarian governance.

Let there be no mistake. The Kargil conflict has brought to the fore the requirements of a wise leadership and a coherent governing arrangement if the Indian state is not to be tested all too often by disrupters at home and abroad; yet, the potential disrupter can be discouraged only if the polity does not abandon its search for an egalitarian social and economic political order. This search is too fundamental to be allowed to be hijacked by the Kargil fever-mongers.

Courtesy: Harish Khare in Hindu, 14.7.1999

VICTORY IN REVERSE

That the Kargil adventure was ill-conceived, if not downright foolish, was becoming clear, albeit slowly, even to the congenitally blind and benighted.

That consequently Pakistan, swallowing its pride and not a few of its brave and gallant words, would sooner or later have to mount a retreat was also becoming clear, especially after Mr. Niaz Naik's secret visit to New Delhi which was a desperate bid to get India to agree to some kind of deal which would provide a face-saving way out for us.

But that the climbdown when it came would be so headlong and ill-judged, and that in the process it would leave in tatters the last shreds of national pride, should take even prophets of doom by surprise. A script written by a college of cynics could not have equalled, let alone excelled, the singular performance of the Heavy Mandate in Washington.

It is not a question of interpreting the hidden meaning of the Washington statement. This statement is a model of clarity which nails Pakistan's humiliation to the mast and leaves nothing to the imagination. If it is still being proclaimed as a great step forward to resolve the Kashmir dispute, it only confirms the view that in Pakistan brazeness is always the last resource of a floundering government.

To repeat the first point, at issue is not Pakistan's retreat. Given the nature of the Kargil adventure, the fact that in planning it the army high command substituted fantasy for a sense of reality, Pakistan had no option but to effect a rollback eventually, whatever armchair Rommels might say to the contrary. As a feint aimed at embarrassing the Indian army, the Kargil operation could have made some sense. As an attempt at permanently occupying the Kargil heights, it was madness if only because no country, whether india or Pakistan, would tolerate such a naked trespass into territory under its control. At issue is the manner of our retreat as agreed to by our great helmsman.

Even when it finally dawned upon Pakistan's Bismarcks and Napoleons that the Kargil intrusion was a blunder, there was no reason to panic. Pakistan still had options before it which, if sensibly exercised, could have brought about a withdrawal with a minimum loss of national dignity. We could have settled matters with Indian and told it that a mistake had been made which we were willing to undo provided (1) there was a scaling down of hostilities along the Line of Control and (2) that India did not make it a point to crow about our discomfiture. This would have been far preferable to the course actually adopted.

But this would have required a measure of statesmanship, a quality of which there has been not the slightest evidence in Islamabad since this crisis erupted. So Pakistan's war leadership did what flowed naturally from its basic instincts: go cap in hand to Washington and agree to an extraordinary statement which commits us to undo our Kargil folly.

A pathetic sop sweetens this mini-Munich: a pledge from the American President that once concrete steps have been taken to restore the Line of Control—that is, once we have undone our folly—, he will take "a personal interest" in encouraging India and Pakistan to resume bilateral discussions. Only a leadership with no idea of national pride and dignity can suppose that an empty pledge such as this is sufficient recompense for the blood of our martyrs.

A more complete negation of Pakistan's stand and a more complete vindication of India's position are hard to envisage. Yet official drum-beaters and Pakistan Television, that weary performer forced to dance to every government's tune; are trying to sell the agreement sealed at Blair House, Washington, as the greatest diplomatic triumph since the Congress of Vienna.

The people of Pakistan are not surprised. They are stunned because this is not what they had been led to expect. The two surprised parties must be Mr. Clinton and Mr. A.B. Vajpayee. When Mr. Nawaz Sharif telephoned Mr. Clinton and requested an urgent meeting, the Amrican President, who is nobody's fool, must have realised in a flash that it was all up with the Pakistanis. But is it far-fetched to suppose that even he must have been taken aback by the eager enthusiasm of the Pakistani leadership to cave in and put its signature to a one-sided document? By the same token, Mr. Vajpayee too must have been taken by surprise. The Indian army, despite the successes it has scored, was not having an easy time of it in Kargil and Dras. Dangerous terrain, an elusive enemy and heavy casualties are not the things an army likes. Imagine then the sense of relief in New Delhi when Mr. Clinton called to say that the Pakistani leadership was about toe execute a volte face and all it demanded in return was that he (Mr. Clinton) should give this turnaround his blessings. A bang turning into a whimper: to this time-worn phrase a fresh meaning has been given.

The Tashkent and Simla accords look like victory parchments by comparison. Ayub Khan did not suffer humiliation at Tashkent. Even if the Tashkent agreement went off badly in Pakistan because official propaganda, always a curse in this country, had raised poplar expectations of fever pitch, it was a fair agreement between the two countries which had fought each other to a standstill. At Simla on the other hand, Pakistan was at a grave disadvantage because it had suffered a humiliating defeat at India's hands. Yet even in the shadow of that disaster, Zulfikar Ali Bhutto, to his enduring credit, managed to preserve what remained of Pakistan's honour. The Washington statement defies understanding. For such submission wherein lay the compelling necessity?

Why has this happened? The answer is simple. Pakistan has suffered a failure of leadership, a failure of vision and, most important of all, a failure of nerve. When the crunch came the politico-military leadership could not take the heat.

Will explanations be demanded for this shambles? It is safe to say 'no' because post-mortems of this kind are not in the Pakistani tradition. The Government's spin machine will go into overdrive, as it has already done, in a bid to paint the Washington capitulation a Roman triumph. The Bismarcks will cover for the Napoleons and the Napoleons for the Bismarcks.

To be sure, Pakistan's fighting men will feel betrayed. The Kashmir cause itself has received a mortal blow. But then who cares? Greater disasters in our history have gone unsung. The humiliation of Kargil too (or is it the humiliation of Washington?) will soon be forgotten.

Even so, is there nothing to be done? To begin with, all the models of the Shaheen and Ghauri missiles, and all the replicas of the Chaghi hills, which adorn our various cities, should be put on board the best of our naval cruisers and, in a solemn midnight ceremony, dumped into the waters of the Arbian Sea. If this crisis has proved anything, it is that the possession of nuclear weapons does not confer immunity against taking stupid decision.

Furthermore, the Prime Minister and the Army Chief, if they can help themselves, should not say anything for a while: no explanations, no brave statements. The people of Pakistan can do without salt being rubbed into their wounds.

Courtesy: Ayaz Amir in
The DAWN Group of Newspapers, 1999